Picture the Past

Life in a Mississippi River Town

Laura Fischer

Heinemann Library
Chicago, Illinois

© 2003 Heinemann Library
a division of Reed Elsevier Inc.
Chicago, Illinois
Customer Service 888-454-2279
Visit our website at www.heinemannlibrary.com

Produced for Heinemann Library by
   Bender Richardson White.
Editor: Lionel Bender
Designer and Media Conversion: Ben White
Picture Researcher: Cathy Stastny
Production Controller: Kim Richardson

07 06 05 04 03
10 9 8 7 6 5 4 3 2 1

Printed and bound by Lake Book Manufacturing, Inc.

Library of Congress Cataloging-in-Publication Data.
Fischer, Laura, 1977-
   Life in a Mississippi River town / Laura Fischer.
      p. cm. -- (Picture the past)
   Summary: An overview of everyday life in the cities of the
central Mississippi River Valley between 1820 and 1870,
when the river was the primary means of transportation.
Includes bibliographical references (p.) and index.
   ISBN 1-4034-3797-1 -- ISBN 1-4034-4283-5 (pbk.)
   1. Mississippi River Valley--Social life and customs--19th
century--Juvenile literature. 2. City and town life--Mississippi
River Valley--History--19th century--Juvenile literature.
3. River life--Mississippi River Valley--History--19th century--
Juvenile literature. (1. Mississippi River Valley--Social life
and customs--19th century. 2. Mississippi River Valley--
History--19th century. 3. City and town life--Mississippi River
Valley--History--19th century. 4. River life--Mississippi River
Valley--History--19th century.) I. Title. II. Series.
   F353.F54 2003
   977'.02--dc21

                                        2003005420

Special thanks to Angela McHaney Brown at Heinemann
Library for editorial and design guidance and direction.

Acknowledgments
The producers and publishers are grateful to the following
for permission to reproduce copyright material:
Corbis Images: cover. Corbis Images/Bettmann Archives,
pp. 8, 13, 20. Corbis Images/Annie Griffiths Belt, p. 30.
North Wind Pictures, pp. 1, 3, 9, 11, 16. Peter Newark's North
American Pictures, pp. 6, 19, 21, 28. The Bridgeman Art
Library: Butler Institute of American Art, Youngstown, OH,
U.S.A., p.23; City Art Museum, St. Louis, MO, U.S.A., p. 25;
Delaware Art Museum, Wilmington, DE, U.S.A., p. 22;
Minnesota Historical Society, U.S.A., p. 18; Museum of the
City of New York, U.S.A., pp. 12, 14; New-York Historical
Society, New York, U.S.A., pp. 10, 24, 26, 27. St. Louis Art
Museum, Missouri, U.S.A., p. 17.

Illustrations by Mark Bergin, p. 15, John James pp. 4, 29,
Gerald Wood, p.7.
Map by Stefan Chabluk.

Every effort has been made to contact copyright holders
of any material reproduced in this book. Omissions will be
rectified in subsequent printings if notice is given to the
publisher.

ABOUT THIS BOOK

This book describes what it was like to live along the Mississippi River between 1820 and 1870. At 2,348 miles (3,779 kilometers) in length, the Mississippi is the second longest river in the United States. The longest is the Missouri River, at 2,466 miles (3,969 kilometers).

At this time, the Mississippi River was the country's main way to transport goods and people. This book focuses mainly on the river towns and cities of the central Mississippi River Valley.

We have illustrated the book with drawings and paintings of people and places along the Mississippi River from this time period. We have also included artists' ideas of how people lived in the 1800s.

The Author

Laura Fischer is a professional writer and editor residing in Chicago, Illinois. She has worked with a variety of online, magazine, and book publishers, and has a special interest in children's literature and nonfiction. She graduated from Michigan State University with a B.A. in English, and is currently working toward an M.A. in elementary education at DePaul University.

Note to the Reader

Some words are shown in bold, **like this.** You can find out what they mean by looking in the glossary.

CONTENTS

A Mighty River 4

Call of the River 6

Towns on the River..........8

Working Towns................10

All Kinds of Boats 12

Steamboats.....................14

River Life 16

Homes 18

Home Life...................... 20

A Child's Day..................22

School.............................24

Clothing 26

Food................................28

River Towns Today........30

Glossary *31*

More Books to Read...... *31*

Index............................. *32*

A Mighty River

The Mississippi River is the country's most important waterway. The area of land around it is called the Mississippi River Valley. The valley is divided into three parts: upper, central, and lower. Between 1820 and 1870, towns and cities developed quickly in the valley. More goods were being shipped on the river than ever before. People moved to the valley to find work. Some workers steered or unloaded the river boats. Other people worked in the growing towns, in stores, businesses, and on farms.

Look for these
The illustration of a Mississippi boy and girl shows you the subject of each double-page story in the book.

The illustration of a Mississippi paddle steamboat marks boxes with interesting facts about life in the central part of the Mississippi River.

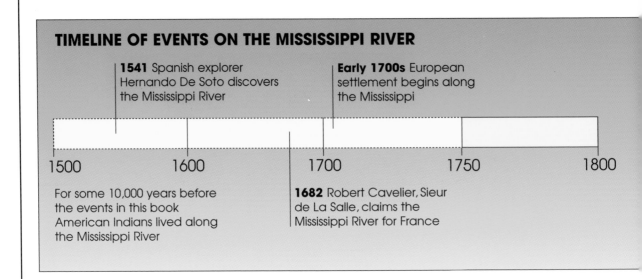

TIMELINE OF EVENTS ON THE MISSISSIPPI RIVER

1541 Spanish explorer Hernando De Soto discovers the Mississippi River

Early 1700s European settlement begins along the Mississippi

1500   1600   1700   1750   1800

For some 10,000 years before the events in this book American Indians lived along the Mississippi River

1682 Robert Cavelier, Sieur de La Salle, claims the Mississippi River for France

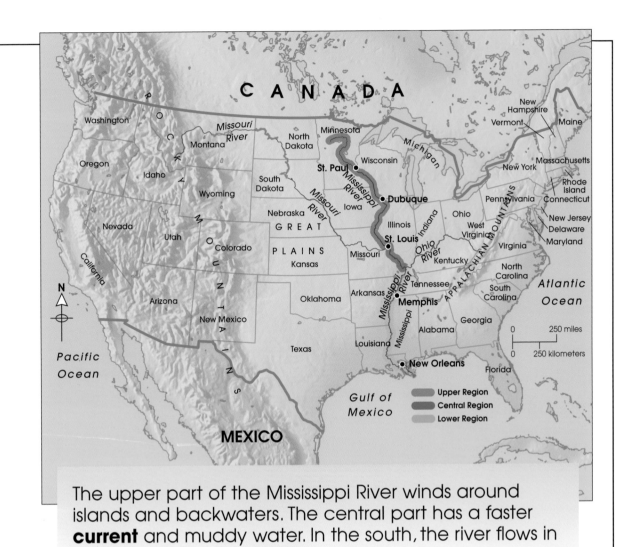

The upper part of the Mississippi River winds around islands and backwaters. The central part has a faster **current** and muddy water. In the south, the river flows in a wide and flat **floodplain.**

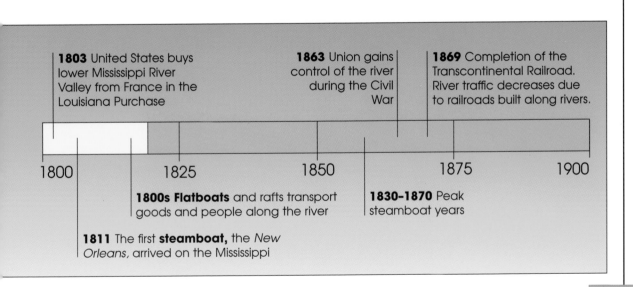

1803 United States buys lower Mississippi River Valley from France in the Louisiana Purchase

1863 Union gains control of the river during the Civil War

1869 Completion of the Transcontinental Railroad. River traffic decreases due to railroads built along rivers.

1800 1825 1850 1875 1900

1800s Flatboats and rafts transport goods and people along the river

1830-1870 Peak steamboat years

1811 The first **steamboat,** the *New Orleans,* arrived on the Mississippi

Call of the River

The river's flowing waters could transport goods and people more quickly than traveling on land. For this reason, towns soon began to form along the river. In the early 1800s, the Mississippi River began to attract settlers from the eastern part of the country. They were looking for new jobs and new land.

Many people traveled to the Mississippi River Valley to set up farms. The **fertile** land was good for farming.

People floating along the Mississippi on rafts built themselves wooden cabins in which to live. They brought only a few belongings with them. They would make or buy most of what they needed when they arrived.

People used horses and covered wooden wagons to move from the East. The trip took two to three months, and it was not easy. Taking care of people, animals, and equipment was hard work. On the last part of the journey, families traveled on open rafts and small boats to reach their new homeland on the river.

NAMING A RIVER

The name *Mississippi* comes from an American Indian word for "big water." *Michi* means "big." *Sippi* means "water."

Towns on the River

Towns formed along the Mississippi where many families settled and built homes. The settlers made buildings of wood, stone, or brick. Wagons, horses, and people traveled on hard dirt roads. The center of town life was the main street. People traveled there to buy supplies and do business. On Saturdays, families would make the trip into town together.

Large river towns were busy places, with stores, saloons, schools, churches, and post offices. Here, in a main street in St. Louis, horsedrawn carts and wagons line the sidewalks.

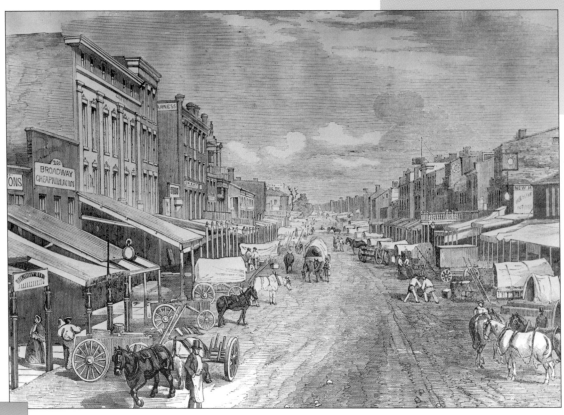

At the **riverfront** were **levees** or **docks.** There, men loaded and unloaded crates of goods from boats on the river. Travelers from the boats shared news with the workers of the town. The docks were noisy, active places. They could be dangerous, too. Workers from the boats were sometimes rough, and often looking for money. The docks could be places of fighting, gambling, and stealing.

Warehouses for storing goods lined the busy riverfront in St. Louis. When a **steamboat** pulled into town, the cry "Steamboat a–comin'!" was shouted from the **wharf.**

Working Towns

The Mississippi River was the nation's most important shipping route. Boats carried products to **docks** in river towns. When the goods reached a dock, workers unloaded them from the boats. Then, the workers divided up the shipments and sent the goods to other towns. The workers sent the shipments by wagons over land, or on other rivers until they were delivered throughout the country.

New Orleans lies near where the Mississippi River flows into the Gulf of Mexico. Ships came from both **upstream** and overseas. Major roads led from the **riverfront,** through the city, to neighboring towns.

River towns shipped and sold goods from all over the country. From the North, river towns received shipments of **livestock** and corn. From the South came tobacco and cotton. Tobacco and cotton were grown on huge farms called **plantations.** Plantation owners used **slaves** to plant and pick the **crops.**

In New Orleans, slaves collected bales—huge bundles —of cotton fibers ready for loading. Each bale weighed more than 400 pounds (180 kilograms).

All Kinds of Boats

For many years, boats used only the wind and the river's **current** to move them. They did not have motors or engines to make them move. In the early days on the Mississippi, **flatboats** were the main source of transportation. They had flat bottoms and floated on the surface of the river. The river's current pushed them **downstream.**

A flatboat makes its way along the river, keeping clear of banks and the huge **steamboats.** Flatboats could only float downstream. They were not able to travel against the current.

One type of flatboat, called a **keelboat,** could travel **upstream.** The front of it was pointed to cut through the water. This type of boat was powered by human strength. People used long poles to push against the bottom of the river. With these poles, they could move the boat upstream against the river current.

To cross the river, people used small keelboats with oars or sails. Here, a steamboat, two big flatboats, and three smaller boats fill a section of the river.

END OF THE ROAD

Flatboats were often taken apart at the end of their journey downstream. It was too hard to take them back against the current. The wood from the boats was used for buildings. The people who worked on the boats walked back overland and floated downriver in new boats.

Steamboats

In 1811, the first **steamboat** traveled on the Mississippi. It was named the *New Orleans.* Steamboats were powered by steam **engines.** These turned big paddlewheels. This meant they could travel **upstream** without the heavy labor. The first people to see the *New Orleans* were amazed. They had never seen a boat like it. Within 20 years, the steamboat had brought major changes to the river.

Slow-speed steamboat races were popular on the Mississippi. The boats would try to beat each other from one city to another. The steamboats shown here had a paddlewheel on each side. Others had one paddlewheel at the back.

This cutaway of a Mississippi River steamboat shows that coal or wood was burned in huge boilers to make steam. The steam powered an engine that turned the paddlewheel. This steamboat had fancy rooms, food, and entertainment for the travelers.

Steamboats made transporting people and goods easier than ever before. Goods from the South could travel upstream to the North in less than half the time it took before. Steamboats also carried people. Traveling by steamboat became very fashionable. Now people could take trips to cities along the river. The Southern city of New Orleans was a popular place to visit.

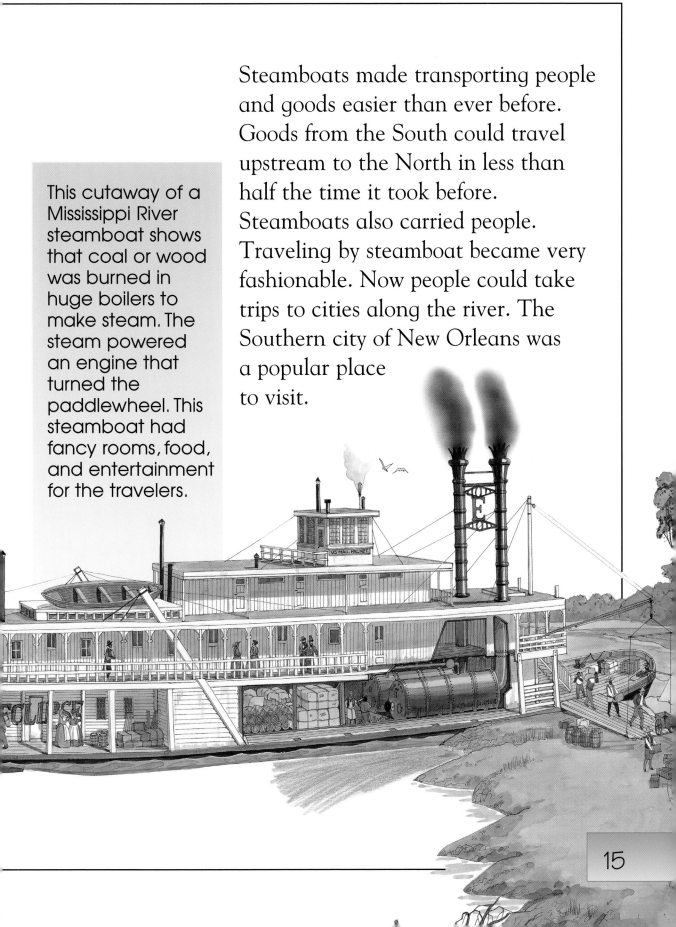

River Life

Many men and some women who lived in river towns and cities had jobs as pilots, captains, or workers on river boats. Often the work was hard and tiring. The Mississippi River can be very rough, with a strong **current.** Pilots had to use a lot of skill to keep their boats on course. They also had to watch out for big rocks, fallen trees, and other boats on the river.

The pilot of a **steamboat** was in charge. He made sure the boat got where it was going safely. This is the pilothouse on the Mississippi River boat *Great Republic.*

MARK TWAIN

A very famous author, Mark Twain, grew up in a Mississippi River town called Hannibal, Missouri. Before he became a writer, he worked as a steamboat pilot. Many of his books, such as *Life on the Mississippi*, *The Adventures of Tom Sawyer*, and *The Adventures of Huckleberry Finn*, describe life on the river.

Workers on steamboats were always busy. Some kept the **engines** running or tied up the boats each time they entered **docks.** Others looked after passengers. In calm stretches of water, workers on **flatboats** and **keelboats** could relax. They played games and sang songs to pass the time.

River boatmen were away from home for weeks at a time. They often became good friends on the boats. Here, workers on a flatboat play cards together.

Homes

Most people in river towns lived in simple wooden houses. Many families built their own homes with logs and boards from trees that grew in the area. Some people lived in houses made of stone or brick. Houses were heated by wood-burning fireplaces. There was no electricity. People used candles and gas lamps for light.

HOUSE-WORK

Homes in river towns did not have such inventions as radios, irons, televisions, computers, telephones dishwashers, or washing machines. All the housework was done by hand. There was much less time for entertainment than there is today.

This house beside the river had a main room, kitchen, and several bedrooms.

The cooking stove was the center of home life. It provided heat and light.

The floors of houses were made of wood. Rugs helped keep the floors warm in winter. Furniture was made of wood, too. In the main room of the house was a big wooden table with wooden chairs or benches where families ate their meals. Homes had no indoor bathrooms. Instead, people went outside to the **outhouse.**

Home Life

CHORE DAYS

Each weekday had its own type of housework. Most women followed this schedule:
Monday—laundry
Tuesday—ironing
Wednesday—sewing
Thursday—cleaning
Friday—baking
Saturday—shopping
Sunday—rest

Workers in river towns would go off to work during the day. Mothers would often stay home and work. There were many chores to do. Women would often clean the house, wash clothes, prepare and cook meals, work in the garden, and sew clothing for their family. Children usually helped their mothers with these chores.

Children learned how to do chores around the house by watching their mothers. This mother is peeling a potato as her daughter watches.

There was as much work to do outside the house as there was inside. Families repaired their own homes when they were damaged by flood or fire. They also built and repaired fences, wagons, and barns. If a family kept chickens or **livestock,** these animals had to be fed and taken care of every day.

A son brings a drink of water to his father, who is tired from cutting logs. Work came first for families. In the evening, after it was done, they would spend time together talking and playing before they went to bed.

A Child's Day

Most children in Mississippi River towns and cities went to school during the day. Before and after school, children did chores at home. They fed the animals and helped clean the house. They picked vegetables in the garden and brought in water from pumps or wells outside. Children helped their parents chop firewood.

A boy and his older sister are about to milk the family's cows before the start of a school day.

Children played outdoor games such as baseball, hide-and-seek, and this game, called crack-the-whip.

Children played with their brothers, sisters, and neighbors. In warm months they swam in the river. Boys usually learned to hunt small animals and practiced shooting guns. Girls often played with rag dolls made by their mothers and practiced sewing. In many ways, children were learning the skills they would need as adults.

AT THE DOCKS

Children would sometimes sneak off to the **docks.** They played there and pretended they were riverboat pilots. Their parents did not like this because the docks could be dangerous places.

School

River town children went to school in one-room schoolhouses. There, children of all ages learned together in the same classroom. Students sat in rows on benches or chairs. Younger students sat in the front of the classroom, and older students sat in the back. There were not a lot of books, paper, and pencils to go around. All students helped clean and take care of the school.

SCHOOL BOOKS

Schools did not have books for every child. Often, students had to bring to school whatever books their family had at home. Using different books made it hard for the teacher to teach his or her lessons. Students wrote on slates that they wiped clean and used again and again.

Students leave their one-room, edge-of-town schoolhouse. Some take their books home to do some extra studies.

Girls often stopped going to school when they were 11 or 12 years old. They stayed home, and their mothers taught them how to take care of a home and family.

Some boys stayed in school until they were 14 or 15 years old, and a few sometimes left home to go to college in a big city. Other boys went to school only in winter. They worked on their family farms during the other seasons.

In class, girls usually sat on one side of the room and boys on the other. They were not supposed to talk or play together in school. There was one teacher for all the lessons. Students were expected to obey their teacher as they would a parent.

Clothing

Women and girls in river towns wore long dresses or skirts and button-down blouses with long sleeves. They never wore pants. There were many layers of clothes to put on. Under their aprons, dresses, and skirts they wore **stockings** and **petticoats.** Women and girls draped a shawl over their shoulders when they went out.

A family, dressed in working clothes of the time, gather round a peddlar—a salesman who went from house to house selling goods. Wealthy people wore more fashionable clothes.

Men and boys wore long cotton or wool pants and shirts that buttoned. When they dressed up, they put on neckties and white shirts. Shoes and boots were made of leather. They cost a lot of money and people kept them until they were worn.

APRONS

Women and girls wore cotton aprons over their dresses to keep their clothes clean. Often the first thing a young girl learned to sew was an apron.

Boys and girls of rich families were dressed in fine clothes to look like adults.

Food

Meals were cooked on wood-burning cook stoves. Common foods of the time were stews, breads, pies, eggs, potatoes, milk, butter, and meat. Many families planted a small garden for fresh vegetables and kept chickens for eggs. In stores or at street markets, women bought the things they could not make or grow, such as flour and sugar.

PUTTING UP

Many women "put up," or **canned,** fruits and vegetables in glass jars to save them for winter when fresh fruits and vegetable were not available.

Families sat down and ate together at every meal. Women spent much of the day cooking.

River Town Recipe—Baking Powder Biscuits

People ate biscuits almost every day. They were a simple and filling type of bread to make and could be eaten at breakfast, lunch, or dinner.

WARNING: Do not cook anything unless a grown-up helps you. Always let a grown-up do the cooking on a hot stove.

YOU WILL NEED
2 cups flour
1 tablespoon baking powder
1 teaspoon salt
1 tablespoon sugar
1/3 cup shortening
1 cup milk

FOLLOW THE STEPS

1. Preheat the oven to 425°F (220°C). In a large bowl, mix together the flour, baking powder, salt, and sugar. Mix in the shortening until the mixture forms large crumbs. Add the milk and stir to combine.

2. Place the dough on a floured surface. Knead it 15 to 20 times with your hands. Pat out the dough to a thickness of 3/4 inch (16 millimeters). Cut out biscuits using a biscuit cutter, empty can, or glass.

3. Place the biscuits on a baking sheet. Bake 13 to 15 minutes or until the biscuits are golden brown. Leave to cool before eating.

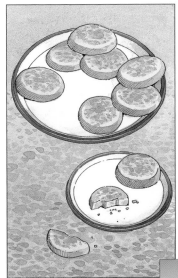

River Towns Today

By the late 1800s, railroad tracks ran across most of the country. Travel by train was fast and cheap. People began to ship many goods by railroad. Because of this, the Mississippi River became a less important transportation route. There was less work for people in river towns. Today, some cities on the Mississippi, such as St. Louis and New Orleans, remain active, busy centers of shipping. Other cities have not grown since the time of the **steamboat.**

Modern St. Louis is a major shipping, business, and tourist city. Here, steamboats carry tourists along the Mississippi, beside the huge Gateway Arch. Tall office and appartment buildings tower over the city center.

Glossary

can to preserve food by heating it to kill germs and sealing it in jars or cans

crop plants that are grown in large amounts for using or selling

current flow of water in a particular direction

dock place where boats can load and unload

downstream the direction a river flows

engine a machine that uses energy to make something move or do work

fertile able to grow crops

flatboat boat with a flat bottom made to carry things on a river

floodplain flat area of land on either side of a river

keelboat boat with a flat bottom and pointed front that moves against the current of a river

levee a river landing place

livestock animals used for work or food, such as cows

outhouse small outdoor building where people go to the toilet

petticoat thin, lightweight skirt worn under a skirt or dress

plantation large farm that used slave labor to raise crops

riverfront area of town that touches a river. Riverfronts are usually busy places with docks, stores, and warehouses.

shawl square piece of fabric worn over the shoulders

slave person who is owned by another person and who is usually made to work for that person

steamboat boat powered by a steam engine

stockings pair of close-fitting leggings worn under dresses and skirts

upstream against the direction a river flows

wharf platform on the water's edge used as a dock

More Books to Read

Fowler, Allan. *The Mississippi River.* Danbury, Conn.: Children's Press, 1999.

Harness, Cheryl. *Mark Twain and the Queens of the Mississippi.* New York: Simon & Schuster, 1998.

Stein, R. Conrad. *The Story of Mississippi Steamboats.* Danbury, Conn.: Children's Press, 1996.

Index

American Indians 4,7
animals 7,21,22,23

books 17,24
buildings 8,13

carts 8
children 20,22–23, 24
churches 8
Civil War 5
clothes 20,26–27
cooking 19,20,28, 29
corn 11
cotton 11
crops 11
currents 5,12,16

docks 9,10,17,23

engines 12,14,15, 17
explorers 4

farms 4,6,25
fireplaces 18
flatboats 5,12,13, 17
floodplain 5
food 15,28–29
furniture 19

goods 4,5,6,9,10, 11,15,26,30

horses 7,8
houses and homes 8,13,18–19,20,21, 22,23
housework 18,20

jobs 6,16

keelboats 13,17

levees 9
livestock 11,21
loading and unloading boats 4,9,10
Louisiana Purchase 5

Mississippi River Valley 4,5,6,11

New Orleans 5,10, 11,15,30

outhouse 19

people (on the move) 4,5,6,7, 13,15,30
pilots 16,17,23

plantations 11
play and games 17,23,25
post offices 8

rafts 5,7
railroads 5,30
river traffic 5
riverfront 9,10
roads 8,10

saloons 8
schools 8,22,24–25
settlers 6,8
sidewalks 8
slaves 11
St. Louis 8,9,11,30
steamboats 5,9, 12,13,14–15,16, 17,30
stores 4,8,28

tobacco 11
Twain, Mark 17

wagons 7,8,10,21
warehouses 9
waterway 4
wharf 9,11
workers 4,9,10,16, 17,20